Things My Mother Taught Me
Sana Booker

Publisher: PenThere.com ©2023

PenThere.com is an independent publishing company committed to supporting new and established writers from all backgrounds. We specialize in publishing works that explore the human experience in all its complexity, from personal memoirs to works of poetry and fiction.
Our mission is to empower writers to share their unique perspectives and stories with the world, and we believe that everyone has a voice that deserves to be heard.

We are honored to have published this book of poems by Sana Booker, and we hope that readers will find inspiration and meaning in its pages. Thank you for choosing PenThere.com as your publisher. We are proud to bring your work to the world.

First Edition

ISBN: 979-8-218-21360-2

Things My Mother Taught Me
Sana Booker

Dedicated to family and many amazing mothers.

-My Family (Ryan, Carl, Cortlan)

-My Mom (Tommie Nolan)

Table of Contents

Poems

Things My Mother Taught Me
Hello Friend
Black Woman Walking
I Need A Win
Older Women
At This Time...
Hey Mom
Where Will You Be?
Joy Of The Day
Built to be Blessed
To Be...
My Love Is...

Prose

She Called Me Ma'am
The Forgotten Ones
Truth

Poems

Things My Mother Taught Me

Believe in God and give Him the glory.

Keep yourself and your surroundings clean and tidy.

Learn everything you can and teach others.

Provide for and protect your family.

Care for those in need.

Go to work without fail.

Do not lie about what you know.

If you say you know it, know it.

Do not tell all of your business to everybody.

If someone will tell you all of their business, they will tell all of yours too.

Avoid the fight if possible, but once in it—win it!

Drunk people say what their sober minds are thinking.

Be a genuine woman, comfortable in your skin always.

Do not mess around with married men, or your friend's man (EVER).

Too thick won't stick (speaks to having someone at your house all the time)

Be respectful, and if not treated with respect end that relationship today.

Laugh every chance you get.

Cook at home and enjoy good food.

When you invite people over to your house for dinner, have the food ready on time.

When something is over, then it is over…leave it alone.

Sing and dance often.

Love with your whole heart.

My mother lived without regrets or apologies. She was the strongest woman I have ever known.

There are many ways that we differed, but the list above has helped me to continue moving forward.

I miss her every day.

Hello Friend

Hello Friend,
It has been such a long time since we sat and talked
Not about other people, places or things—
         just about us.
Remember when we would chat about our future for hours
we laughed about silly subjects and our own mistakes
Then we moved on without looking back.
Seems like we had endless energy
No aches or breaks that now distract from fun and smiles.
I remember when just us two could make a party
that others wanted to join—
Where did those times go?
I miss the us we use to be
Let's get it back, you and me,
         Your place or mine?
Hello Friend…

Black Woman Walking

Black Woman Walking…..
Today is the day for speaking truth,
Head up, feet planted
Saying "No" without explanation
Hairstyle just might be braids, fro, straight or
Shaved bare…blowing here or there
Still without explanation or permission
Yeah, she knows that she is too beige, brown, or black to go unnoticed
Heard someone comment on her walk, laugh, and talk
Watched her coming and going, and still confused
Why is she here, where did she come from?
A little too proud for regular entitled taste,
But pleasant enough for polite company,
… Unless it became necessary to state her case, administer some grace
Stand in the gap
Conjugate that rap—to be clear
She is a Black Woman Walking…

I Need A Win

I need a win
Not a little one or in between, but a big one where my ship comes in
I need a win…
Maybe a solid hit out of the park,
Or at least out of reach
When I am walking in light
But unafraid of the dark…yes I need a win…
I want a lot, not just enough to get by,
More to give than a pittance
Want to make it and not try
I want a win….
I want the stars to align, and to feel brand new
How about a win..just one, maybe two?
I could use a win, not tomorrow but today
Just 24 hours of things going my way….

What about you, do you need a win?
When your best is great, when your dreams come true
When you are blessed to breathe and your mind works too
You have friends you can laugh with and family to stand by
Or memories of love that still causes you to sigh…..but
When I think it all over and look back at my life
Been a daughter, a friend, a mother and wife
I can see God's grace holding steady and true
So let's call them all wins…more than one or more than two…

Older Women

Often overlooked, cause youngins don't know
Where she has been or where she will go…
if stepped to wrong
She is seen in the past,
In black and white
She has lived through wrong, and can recognize right
But she knows how to hold her words

She has been walked away from
Left behind some, and though she was loved, or could have been
She stopped settling for boyfriends or now and thens
Cause she is all out or all in

Seasoned, mature, broad or dame
Mrs., Ms, all the same cause she
Worked for it, earned it, babies, husbands, others and lovers
Now stronger, straighter, tolerant, but no foolishness allowed
Younger women would do themselves proud
If they leaned on and learned from…the older woman

At This Time

Life has been playing us hard of late.

It has been running through my mind that these feel like biblical days of trials and tribulations.

I guess that this season should not be surprising, after we have lost ourselves in reality TV, and the "it feels good at the moment, let's try this new thing and see what happens attitude" that keeps us stimulated.

Expecting a pandemic is a bit much, but we should have seen the demonstration of hatred become overt and comfortable for many.

Lies masked as weak truths and life and death played out like horror movies. All of this can make most days seem heavier…

But still we are a sturdy lot.

We bury our dead and forge ahead in the fight for right, no matter the cost. Speaking the truth loud and clear while stepping up to the plate to swing again for justice.

Undeniably stronger than we ever imagined, though sometimes unsteady and sad, we can find a smile or even laughter while we love, hope and stay the course.

Yes, life has been dealing some challenging hands, but we are built to withstand the torrent rushing us.
Not to be messed with, it will not get too hard for us to continue to stand.

We are survivors, warriors, and believers so we hold on..

Hey Mom....

It was a rough year
I took some losses, some clean others not so much
Walked away from what did not work for me, but still felt hurt
It was a rough year.
Plans fell through, money too, but life moves on as it is apt to do
We talked Mom, did some laughing, dreamed some dreams, and
I said to myself it's not as bad as it seems...but
It was a rough year.
Trusting in the plan God has can be hard when the light is dim,
Not trusting is harder when your life is not right.
It sure was a hard year.
A bit more battered and smarter by far I could finally see the light of my star
A change in the atmosphere, a shift in the view
It was a hard year, but I made it through.

Where Will You Be?

Where?
Where will you be my friend
When the lines are drawn, and the truth is told
Will you stand with me or be hard to see—
Where will you be?
We have built a relationship on trust, but I still must wonder
If you will show up when the winds of time forever change
The historical doubt that weighs in the rear of my mind ask the question
Where will you be?
Life can bend our backs and break our spirits
It can allow constituents to look like friends until the tide comes in,
So, I wonder if you are real or faux, hard to know, 'til I can see
Where you will be.

Joy Of The Day

It is a new year and I promised myself that I would be softer in my spirit—

To look over and past the ridiculous and inane

Every morning as the new day begins I am prayerful that I can keep my bad nerves in check and my thoughts focused on positive blessings.

It can be a struggle to hear the daily news, office politics and the chit chat about the state of relationships, leadership, and broken promises, but

If I can remember the power of words to build and encourage, recall the great friendships that have inspired and stood in the gap for me over and over again

Lest I forget my failures that have been the foundation for my best come backs

Yes, this is how I can quietly, and with reverence, feel the joy of the day

Built to be Blessed

You have handled most of the challenges that life has thrown your way.
Some mountains were harder to climb than others, but you always knew.
Even when you were scared and wanted to run away, when it was hard to laugh, but you did it anyway. Because you knew.
Remember those times when your back was against the wall,
And your set-backs seemed to go on forever
You would put your heart out there once again, for one more hit and maybe a win
Another maybe and this time yes…, because you knew
You knew the truth about who you believed in and the faith that has carried you through it all.
You knew the outcome would be in your favor, that you were covered in grace, and
Built to be blessed…

To Be...

The longing for more...
For change-something new
The constructional cracks in your soul seen by you.
Thinking about time running out. To old, to slow, unheard, unseen
Questioning everything and everyone, but especially yourself with what ifs, should haves, and could have been.
Replaying old failures that worked out for the good, if you look out far enough or back at the facts.
Trying to find and hold on to solid footing when the feeling of drifting away keeps creeping in.

But what if...

The old spiritual that says to "grip the solid rock" really works.
My friend said to "tie a knot at the end of your rope and hold on" help is on the way.
The bible says that "our present troubles are small and won't last long". Trust in God for everything.
The only choice is to believe that tomorrow makes for a new beginning...that yesterday was training for the good to come.
The strongest are challenged to stand in the gap for those who need the most help, and your come back is one moment away.

So maybe you are stronger than you think.

That big hurt, mistake, and stumble is but a passing memory in your future.
God does know all about the outcome so breathe in and out, smile at old memories, and begin again to be you.

My Love Is..

Too powerful to be met with indifference, laziness and coldness
To passionate be held prisoner inside myself without release or response
To original to be treated as something ordinary or mediocre
To lasting to be given to a short-term, part-time recipient
To faithful to be trusted with a double-mind and low character
To present to receive remnants of someone's past lessons
To potent to be defined by age and change
My love has a destination, an unlimited capacity for growth
It offers shelter from the storms of life and it is an intercessory in times of darkness
My love is mine to give and it offers a return on the investment of one who gives back
Do not accept it if you are not going to value and protect it
My love is a verb and a noun…a powerful combination

Prose

Truth

Truth is a scary thing. It comes in so many forms, and voices. It shows up at the most inopportune time and often uninvited. It can leave a taste in your mouth and a memory in your mind that can last a lifetime. We all say that we value the truth, but if the truth be told, a lie sometimes swallows easier and it can feel warm and fuzzy inside, at least for a little while.

The truth is not always warm and fuzzy, and it comes with lumps and bruises. It can weather storms, battles and wars while holding steady. Truth does not bend or break, and it is waterproof, fireproof and time tested. The truth dares you to take it on, and even on trembling legs it is a dangerous adversary.

The old saying that the truth will set you free is real. What it does not say is that sometimes you do not want that freedom. You would rather live with that comfortable, safe, lie. It feels okay to keep your head in the sand, and your eyes averted. It is easier for your family, church members and co-workers if everything looks good on the outside; if life moves on with business as usual. Then quietly without so much as an introduction "truth" strolls in and delivers a, take your breath away, blow. The truth, while usually told with few words, can straighten your back, clear your vision, and turn you into a grown man or woman on the spot.

The truth ain't no joke, but it can be funny. Like when your best girlfriend says "girl that dress does not go with any part of your body". You might get mad for a moment, but you know that she is telling the truth so you laugh, and take the dress back to the store. More often than not the truth is more like a shot of whiskey than a sip of wine. It is what is left when all of the layers are removed. Yeah, it is scary alright, but then again it comes with power.

Truth and power go hand in hand. When the truth is the first level of defense then the offense better come strong or go home. When the truth is in harmony it can be sung acapella with every note on key. When truth is in you then you are selective with friends, and associates. The truth is the core of strong families, churches and businesses. The truth can break hearts and mend wounds. It is the foundation that builds hope and gives light during dark seasons. It can find its way home and start over again. It can offer second, third and fourth chances, or it can give you the strength to walk away. Yeah, truth is scary but it proves easier in the end.

The Forgotten Ones

They were fathers, mothers, daughters and sons, friends and lovers, until this time…when they outlived or outlasted relationships, or the interest of the "very" busy, or the disengaged. They often sit and stare, locked into a world of silence. Sometimes they talk or sing out loud to an imaginary someone who seems to listen and maybe responds.

Their bodies and hearts still feel joy and need love and care, but so much is locked inside. The need to express comes out as snappy retorts and tears of frustration.
They are the forgotten ones.

Left behind, with no voices or choices. Curled into unnatural positions, often not understanding all of the hustle and bustle that surrounds them… strangers rush by,
providing for immediate needs, but rarely with enough time to spend time showing care.
Underpaid and unappreciated workers give what they can, but they can barely invest in these old and sick strangers who are moving closer to the end.
They too are the forgotten ones.

But maybe, if just for a moment, we take a closer look at the forgotten ones, we might just see ourselves. Our passing days amongst semi-familiar faces. Distant places in our minds still remembered. Maybe we will think of joyful times filled with laughter or perhaps, there be no memories at all….and then we will be forgotten.

The Forgotten Ones are still here, breathing in and out. They are still part of the greater good, sum total, and are to be counted. They are memories of other days and contributors to the life we live.

They were us… but we are them, before they became The Forgotten Ones…

She Called Me Ma'am

I am not sure why this hit me so hard. After all I am 58 years old and well past being grown so why did a little teasing about the gray in my hair give me pause. It is not like the gray was a surprise since I decided to never color my hair. The women in my family do not gray early and when we do it is a lovely silver that will wear well in a short do. My plan is to let it gray completely and then get a really sharp short cut to accent the silver strands. This is the plan, and I am sticking to it, but still the teasing from a friend, who is grayer than I am, caught me off guard. We laughed and I gave him a little tap on the shoulder, but I thought about it.

A week or so later the hit came when a young lady said "thank you ma'am" when I wished her a good day. Well if the truth be known I had been looking at myself and seeing all of the bulges, wrinkles, and battle scars of just living. I have passed the age of catching eyes and even my husband has settled into a comfortable state of indifference. Unfortunately, women never stop wanting to be wanted or noticed, and when we accept that maybe that time has passed we still long for those days of a little stare and a nod hello.

I have been married a long time and I am the mother of two amazing young men. I have a best friend and I had a great dog for 13 years. There have been some severe bumps in the road and others that are the cycle of life, but for the most part my life is following an expected pattern of regularity. Still there is that inner voice that speaks to my soul. It makes me think 30 years younger and dream of the feeling of butterflies and loving sighs. It clutches my heart when I hear an old love song and I remember how I looked and felt back then. I carry these thoughts around and for a time and it becomes easy to forget that it is not 30 years earlier. I feel young, vibrant, sassy, and funny. Even my steps, when my knee does not hurt, has a pep to it reminiscent of years past. These feelings go on until I am reminded that in the here and now no one sees that woman any more. I am sought out for advice because I am considered a woman of wisdom. I have skills, and experiences that can prove valuable in different situations. I now fit into a certain niche and admittedly sometimes that can be pretty cool. Thankfully I have lived long enough to see history repeat itself, and to know the end of the story before the beginning is barely told. There is no reason for me to be this old and still be dumb, but there are still moments. (sigh)

Then I recall that this is the time of life when I am mom to adults, grandmom, wife, daughter, church member, and worker. I accept these titles with a "yeah I have been there and done all of that" attitude. There have been stumbles and falls, but the get-up and the comebacks have been amazing. I have watched God bless me, mine, and others over and over again, and when He brought us out He brought us better.

Just for the record, this 50+ woman wants romance, love, passion, attention, and maybe a rendezvous (just mentioning). I still dream and imagine myself as a sensuous 20-year-old but with the mind of a woman who has lived some. I love my family, friends and all the other blessings of my life, but if for a moment I could feel the newness of falling in love and being loved again I would be revitalized. Maybe these are just my feelings. Maybe other 50+ women have found that place of satisfaction or they have that feeling of passion, laughter, and other stuff. So if that be true, I applaud you, and though I am a little jealous, I say with enthusiasm…you go girl!!!!

Sana G. Booker is a writer, public servant, consultant, wife, and mother of two adult children. She owns and operates SG Booker Consulting, LLC, was elected the first City Clerk of West Lafayette, IN in November 2015, and has been an active member of the community for many years. She holds a bachelor's degree in political science and a master's degree in human resource management. Mrs. Booker has served on the West Lafayette Board of Public Works and Safety since 2009, working to improve, maintain, and develop the city she calls home. In addition to her public service, Mrs. Booker is an avid writer and bases her style on experience and reflection. She has a passion for social justice and community engagement. Mrs. Booker enjoys spending time with her family and friends, learning new things, and exploring her faith. She has a contagious sense of humor and loves to laugh and share her gifts with the world.

www.ingramcontent.com/pod-product-compliance
Lightning Source LLC
Chambersburg PA
CBHW042342150426
43196CB00001B/21